Kaw City
A PICTORIAL HISTORY

ANNETTE PITTMAN
SUSAN RUTLEDGE

With Love
Annette Pittman

WILLOW
BEND
PRESS

Published by Willow Bend Press, Prosper, TX

willowbendpress.com

Hardcover ISBN-13: 978-1-950019-13-7

Paperback ISBN-13: 978-1-950019-12-0

First Printing, May 2019

Authors: Annette Pittman and Susan Rutledge

susanrutledge@mac.com

Publisher's Cataloging-in-Publication Data

Names: Pittman, Annette, author. | Rutledge, Susan, author.

Title: Kaw City – a pictorial history / by Annette Pittman and Susan Rutledge

Description: Includes index. | Prosper, TX: Willow Bend Press, 2019.

Identifiers: ISBN 978-1-950019-13-7 (Hardcover) | 978-1-950019-12-0 (pbk.)

Subjects: LCSH Kaw City (Okla.)--Pictorial works. | Kaw Lake Region (Okla.)--Pictorial works. | Kaw Lake (Okla.)--Pictorial works. | Kay County (Okla.)--Pictorial works. | Oklahoma--History--20th century. | BISAC HISTORY / United States / State & Local / Southwest (AZ, NM, OK, TX)

Classification: LCC F701 .P58 2019 | DDC 976.6/053--dc23

In loving memory of Robert William "Bob" Cline
October 8, 1925-January 31, 1989

Preface

My parents, Bob and Annette Cline, began talking, planning and actively pursuing the preservation of Kaw City's history over five decades ago. Having both grown up in Kaw, their passion was deeply rooted in the rich heritage they witnessed and experienced as children. They borrowed and spent countless hours copying hundreds of photographs from Kaw City residents, some who had moved across the country after the town was turned over to the Corps of Engineers. At their own expense, they paid for all the equipment, film, developing and shipping. It was a huge and costly undertaking.

My dad died in 1989, but mom and other family members carried on the vision. The end goal was to make the historical collection available to the public. In 2018, two of their great grandchildren, Madelyn Ray and Nicholas Ray began digitizing every photograph, documenting all the notes attached to each one. The images have been numbered and organized into a system designed to allow searching and easy access at the Kaw City Museum.

I make no apologies for the quality of the pictures. They are old. Many were discovered in attics and basements...and it shows. They were copied "as is" and treasured despite their flaws. Digitally altering, though possible, but would have removed their charm and authenticity. I hope you will enjoy them just the way they are as much as I have.

~Susan Rutledge

Every effort has been made to accurately name people, businesses, locations and dates. Old documents, headstones, obituaries and newspaper articles, along with first, second and third-hand memories have been among the resources used to compile the historical information in this book.

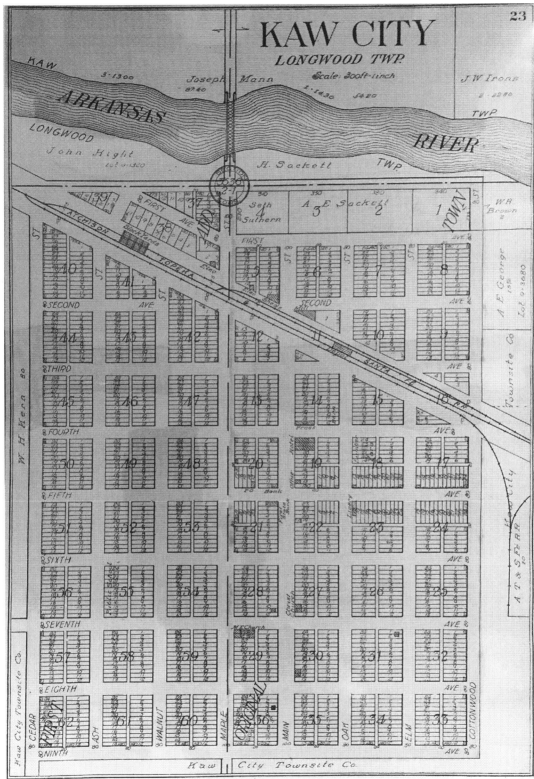

Photo courtesy of Library of Congress, Geography and Map Division

Map of Kaw City (1910)

This early map of Kaw City comes from a Kay County Atlas. It shows numbered lots and blocks, streets, some buildings, the railroad and the Arkansas River.

Guy Family Picture (1868)

The Guy family (L-R): Lissa Guy, Dorinda Guy *(mother)* holding Nora Guy, Homer E. Guy, Jesse Milton Guy *(father)* and Alice Guy. Homer grew up and built Kaw City's first mill.

Cattle Drive (Circa 1870s)

Jim Clubb *(third from right)* having dinner at the chuckwagon after a long day of herding cattle. The well-known western photographer W.S. Prettyman snapped this picture as he accompanied the wranglers on their cattle drive.

Farmers (1872)

This is an early day farm scene taken near Kaw City.

Ike Clubb and Friend (1883)
Young cowboy, Ike Clubb *(left)* worked cattle in the Cherokee Outlet. He is holding a Merwin & Hulbert revolver, seated next to a friend who is holding a single-action Colt revolver. Years later, Ike became a wealthy cattle owner and Kaw City businessman.

Log Cabin in Cherokee Outlet (Circa 1890s)
This log cabin was likely built by settlers who came to Oklahoma Territory in the Cherokee Strip Land Run of 1893.

Cherokee Strip Land Run (1893)

The Cherokee Strip Land Run began at noon on September 16, 1893 with the shot of a cannon. These people have come with their wagons and horses to get their place in line. It is reported that more than 100,000 people raced to claim one of the 42,000 parcels of land up for grabs in Oklahoma's fourth and largest land run. Under the Homestead Act of 1862, settlers could claim 160 acres of public land and receive title to it in five years if they lived on the land and improved it.

Early Day Hunter (Late 1800s)
Many people survived in the early days by hunting. This man displays fur skins from a hunting trip.

Ferguson Family (Late 1800s)

This is a typical family photograph from the late 1800s. People were somber and often looked away from the camera. (R-L): John and Mary Ellen Ferguson *(seated)* with their children Margaret Ferguson Heffron, Henry Ferguson, William A. Ferguson and wife, Eva Ferguson.

Early Settler Dugout (1894)

Dugouts were shelters built at least partially underground or in the side of a hill or ravine. They were often the first dwelling for settlers, offering affordable protection from the weather. This early settler dugout was built near Blackwell in 1894 for a total cost of $3.60.

Courtesy of R. W. Cline

Crossing the Arkansas River (1895)
Arthur Smith *(left)* crosses the Arkansas River with Mr. and Mrs. J.W. DeCou in a canoe. They settled in the Kaw City area after the Cherokee Strip Land Run of 1893.

West Side School House (Circa 1900)

The West Side School was a white frame schoolhouse built on Acker Hill, west of where Kaw City would soon be built. Most of these children came to the area with their families during the Cherokee Strip Land Run of 1893.

Clyde Sharp (Circa 1903)

Early day sheriff Clyde Sharp *(right)* ran a livery stable in Kaw City. The fancy buggy he escorted young women to events in made him quite popular with the ladies. Pictured center front is Irene Diamond.

EAST 5TH AVE KAW OKLA-

Photo courtesy of Lillian Brill

Kaw City Townsite Company (Early 1900s)

This may be one of the only photographs of the Kaw City Townsite Company where W.J. Krebs set up shop to sell lots to the early settlers of Kaw City. Pictured on the right, this office would have been in the Fifth Avenue side of the Bank of Commerce Building.

Bert Fleharty (1902)
Young Bert Fleharty stands between a pony and a mule. His parents were some of the earliest Kaw City settlers.

Railroad Gang (1902)
A group of men who built the railroad in the early 1900s.

Waiting for the Ferry (Circa 1902)

Before the river bridges were built, people depended on a ferry to cross from one side of the Arkansas River to the other. These people wait on the dock for their turn to ride and cross.

Building the Bridge (1903)

Workers are driving pilings as they work on the construction of the railroad bridge across the Arkansas River. This was the only bridge leading in and out of Kaw City that survived all of the floods.

Pellman Chickens (Early 1900s)

G.H. Pellman and family advertise their Orphington chickens. The Orphingtons were a specific breed named after Orphington, England where they were first developed. The chickens were bred for superior egg laying.

Main Street (Circa 1904)

Kaw City was two years old in this photograph. Buildings were quickly springing up along Main Street. The railroad crossing sign at the far north end of town *(center back)* indicates the railroad line had been completed.

Taylor Bar (Circa 1905)

The Taylor Saloon, owned by John Henry Taylor, was one of the early businesses in Kaw City. It was likely impacted in 1907 when Oklahoma became a state and prohibition was enacted.

Cox Wedding (1903)

This wedding portrait, typical of those taken in the early 1900s, is of Eva Ferguson Cox and William Cox on their wedding day, June 10, 1903. Eva was the aunt of Dora Furgeson Cline.

Headed to Town (Early 1900s)
Early Kaw City family crossing the bridge as they head into town on their horse-drawn wagon.

Farm Machinery (Early 1900s)

Farmers harvesting crops outside of Kaw City.

Threshing Fields (Early 1900s)

Women rarely worked in the fields and especially not while wearing dresses. These women probably came to bring food to the farmhands.

Kaw City Main Street (Circa 1904)

Covered wagons and horses were the mode of transportation in the early 1900s. This view of Main Street looking north gives a good view of Ben Smith's Hardware Store next to Lewis Drugs. Once this building was built, B.H. Smith sent for his family to join him. They arrived on December 21, 1902 and took up residence in Kaw City. The Bank of Commerce of Kaw City is seen on the corner, next to the drugstore.

Blacksmith DeBolt (Circa 1906)

Blacksmiths heat different kinds of metals in a forge to prepare them for shaping with hand tools. Warren DeBolt, wearing a heavy protective leather apron, stands in front of his Blacksmith Shop in Kaw City.

Hotel Herman (1903)

The Hotel Herman was one of the first hotels in Kaw City. T.E. Smith had his first Dry Goods Store in the right half of the first floor of the building. Hotel Herman was later named the Santa Fe Hotel.

Kaw City Train Depot (Early 1900s)

Built in 1902, the Depot building was originally much larger than it is today. After WWII the freight room and loading dock visible in this picture were torn down.

W.J. Krebs and Family (Circa 1902)

Front (L-R): W.J. Krebs *(Father)*, Suzie Krebs, Gladys Krebs, Mrs. Krebs *(Mother)* and Paul Krebs. Back (L-R): Ella Krebs, Bill Krebs, John Krebs and Ester Krebs. W.J. was in charge of selling lots for the Kaw City Townsite Company and owned the first newspaper.

PUBLIC SCHOOL   KAW OKLA

Photo courtesy of Lillian Brill

Kaw City's Second School House (1904)
This two-story school house was built in 1904. It was located two blocks west of the city's first school house which was a one-room building that was outgrown after just two years.

Ruby Irons (Early 1900s)

Ruby grew up to be an accomplished pianist, studying and performing in New York City. She moved back to Kaw City to care for her sick mother and taught piano lessons in a second-floor studio above the Bank of Kaw City.

Early Days on Main Street (Early 1900s)
This photograph of Kaw City, likely taken prior to Oklahoma becoming a state in 1907, is a view of Main Street looking south.

Clyde Sharp Livery

Clyde Sharp's Livery, Feed and Stable lodged and rented horses and buggies. Clyde Sharp stands on the right, holding two of the horses.

Photo courtesy of Lillian Brill

First Methodist Church (1904-1912)
Lightning struck the First Methodist Church steeple in 1912 and the church burned to the ground. The congregation moved to a building the Presbyterian Church was no longer using and remained there until 1925 when their new building was completed.

Photo courtesy of John Krebs

W.J. Krebs Newsroom (Circa 1902)

W.J. Krebs began the town's first newspaper shortly after Kaw City's inception. Krebs *(center back)* is talking with an itinerant printer. Charles Spencer *(seated)* later bought the paper from Mr. Krebs.

Bank of Commerce (Early 1900s)

The Bank of Commerce was originally a wooden 2-story building, built in 1902 at the corner of Main Street and Fifth Avenue. In 1909, plans to build a new 2-story brick building were announced. In June of that year, the wooden building was moved into the intersection where it remained open for business until the new brick building could be built.

Barnum Family (Circa 1900)
Pearl Annis Barnum posed with her father for Kaw City Photographer, Mr. Bandholtz.

Photo courtesy of Jack Kneedler

Randoll Livery (1908)

Livery stables were historically the place to rent horses, wagons and buggies. Frank Randoll owned and operated Randoll Livery in Kaw City.

Photo courtesy of John Hoefer

W.T. Conklin Grain Company (1908)

W.T. "Bill" Conklin built and operated the grain elevator in Kaw City for many years. He is standing on the left side of the elevator next to his wife Mary Ellen Diamond Conklin and their children Floyd and Ellen Conklin.

Out For a Walk (1906)
(L-R): Mary Ellen Diamond, Harley Taylor, Ada Gray, Myrtle St. Clair, Mabel Yeoman, Susie Krebs and Bill Krebs out for a walk near the north bridge. For entertainment, people often came to the north end of town to watch one of the trains come in.

The Wedding Gift (1909)

On October 12, 1909, James Ellsworth Neill presented a buggy and horse, Prince, as a wedding gift to his new wife Maude Stough Neill. The Neill Cottage is visible in the background.

Home of W.T. and Mary Ellen Conklin (Circa 1907)
This home was originally built in 1902 for Governor Jenkins, the Fifth Territorial Governor of Oklahoma Territory. Jenkins was part of the Kaw City Townsite Company that established the town.

Photo courtesy of Lillian Brill

Kaw City Main Street (Circa 1908)

Few photographs of downtown Main Street were taken from the vantage point of the residential area. The southern part of Main Street from this point backwards contained several blocks of homes.

Millinery Shop (Circa 1905)
Augusta Graham owned and operated this hat store which supplied Kaw City women with hats for every occasion. Augusta, who later married Jim Clubb, hand made all of the hats she sold.

Kaw City Post Office (Circa 1903)
This building on Main Street was the first Post Office in Kaw City. Postmistress Myrtle Hughes stands in front. It later moved to Fifth Avenue.

B.F. "Bill" Smith Hardware Store (Circa 1905)
Bill Smith stands behind the counter on the right in his Hardware Store.

Photo courtesy of Gladys Yoeman

Eighth Grade Student Class Picture (1908)
Front (L-R): Lulu Gingerich, Blanche Mann, Mary Peterson and Vangie Elwell. Back (L-R): Iral Fleharty, Henry Nelson and Gladys Krebs.

Early Day Transportation (Circa 1903)
Opal Wolfe and Edna Morgan are out for a drive in a horse-drawn carriage.

Conklin Opera House (1904)

W.T. Conklin *(center)* stands in front of his new building. The stairway on the right leads up to the opera house entrance. Brothers Mose Conklin *(left)* and Min Conklin *(right)* operated a store on the lower level. They sold sewing machines, dry goods, guns clocks, etc.

First Christian Church (Early 1900s)

The First Christian Church was one of the first churches in Kaw City. It faced west on Main Street at the southern end of the businesses. The large steeple above the front door had to be removed a few years later, possibly due to a lightning strike.

H.E. Guy Home (1910)

Wall paper, rugs and ornate woodwork added to the charm of some of the beautiful homes in Kaw City. The Guys moved to Kaw City from Bloomfield, Iowa and helped settle the new town. Visible on the back wall is a pennant from Kaw City High School.

First State Bank of Kaw City (1909)

The First State Bank of Kaw City was organized in 1909 and announced plans to build a new $7,000 two-story brick building on Main Street, replacing the frame building the bank started out in when it first opened as The Bank of Commerce *(1902)*. Five years after its inception and two years before it became First State Bank of Kaw City, the name changed to First National Bank of Kaw City *(1907)*. In 1911, it became Farmer's National Bank. In 1920, it became First National Bank in Kaw City, and in 1965, the bank moved to Ponca City and became Pioneer National Bank.

Clubb Ranch (Early 1910s)

Ike Clubb stands proudly displaying some of the Arabian Horses he raised on the Clubb Ranch.

Early Day Home (Early 1900s)

Dining room from the early 1900s, typical for the time period. Often special dishes and other mementos were displayed on plate rails hung high on the walls.

Bandstand (Circa 1911)

The Kaw City Band furnished many entertaining performances for the community from the gazebo bandstand at Fifth Avenue and Main Street. Citizens would bring chairs to sit and enjoy the music.

Ortho and Maxine Harvey (1915)
Big brother Ortho taking his younger sister Maxine on a wagon ride.

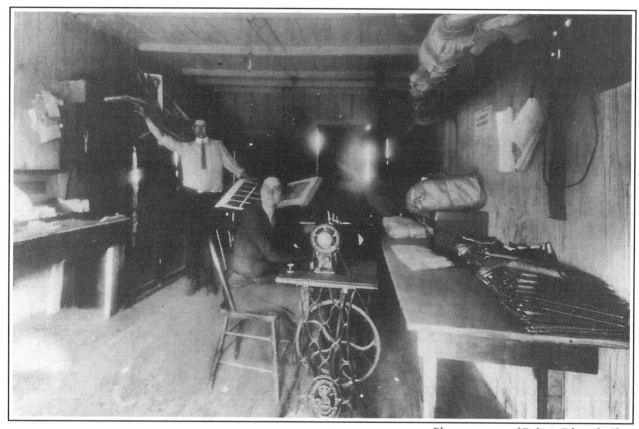

Edwards Tailor and Cleaning Shop (Circa 1910s)
Standing is owner Sylvan Edwards. Seamstress Beatrice Muir Edwards, his daughter-in-law, is seated at the sewing machine.

Edwards Tailor and Cleaning Shop (Circa 1910s)
The photographer's reflection is visible in the display case as he takes a picture of Sylvan and Everett Edwards. Fashion posters on the wall highlight current styles.

Moving the Hay (Circa 1910s)

Harvesting and bailing hay in the early 1900s was hot, hard work. Without the modern day machinery that was invented decades later, this farmer has rigged up a manual pulley device to grab hay and load the horse drawn wagon.

Photo courtesy of Lillian Brill

Kaw City Main Street (Circa 1910s)
Main Street view of Kaw City looking south towards the residential area of town. The bell tower of the Christian Church is visible at the end of the left side of the businesses.

Main Street Garage (Circa 1910s)

Albert L. Lyon was one of the automobile mechanics at Main Street Garage, located at the north end of Main Street.

Kenner Family (Circa 1910s)
Bart Kenner was one of the first Kaw City Sheriffs. Standing (L-R): Leona, Jim, Bob and Edgar. Seated (L-R) Bart, Owen and Mrs. Kenner.

Farmers National Bank of Kaw City (1911)
In 1911, 1st State Bank of Kaw City became Farmers National Bank of Kaw City, then The First National Bank in Kaw City in 1920, before changing hands and moving to Ponca City as Pioneer National Bank in 1965.

Photo courtesy of John E. Hoefer, Jr.

Farmers National Bank of Kaw City (1911)
John E. Hoefer, Sr., standing in front of the bank, was the President of Farmer's National Bank in 1911.

Photo courtesy of Emma Early

First Methodist Church (1912-1925)

The Presbyterian Church was the first congregation to worship in this building but as time passed, it dissolved. In 1912, First Methodist's congregation took over the building after theirs was hit by lightning and burned. They moved out *(1925)* when their new building was completed and a Baptist congregation, pastored by Rev. Calhoon, moved in. Years later, the building was purchased by the American Legion.

Photo courtesy of Glen Conklin

Kaw City Military Band (1911)
Back (L-R): Director Mr. George Kelley, Bill Krebs, Cleo Jenkins, Glen Grantham, Ben F. Smith, Moses Bellmard, Earl Herman and Dennis Alego. Middle (L-R): Harold Kelley, Unknown , Dr. J.T.B. Widney, Tommie Smith, Lren Scott, W.H. "Bill" Smith and John Krebs. Front (L-R): Ed Lewis, W.A. Shidler, Mrs. Ed (Pearl) Lewis, Edna Morgan Feagins, Unknown, and Leon Ervin.

Feagin's Drugstore (Circa 1915)
Clarence Feagin and Fred Seibert stand behind the soda fountain counter at Feagin's Drugstore.

Photo courtesy of Glen Conklin

Kaw City Depot (1917)
People came early and waited for the train to arrive so they could greet friends and loved ones. Because it was 1917, the train may have been bringing WWI soldiers home.

Armstrong Restaurant and Rock Island Machine Shop (1912)
Many of the early Kaw City photographs show men posing in their fancy new automobiles. Somone marked this photograph with an arrow by the phone pole to point out Bill Krebs who is seated in the back seat of the car *(right)*. This is one of the rare photographs showing the Armstrong Restaurant and Rock Island Machine Shop.

Mrs. Dossett and Friends (Circa 1916)

Hats came in many shapes and sizes and a well-dressed woman never left home without one. Mrs. Dossett *(left)* poses with her fashionable Kaw City friends.

Cement Block Factory (1911)
C.F. Kneedler Sr. and C.F. Kneedler Jr. in front of C.F. Kneedler & Sons Block Factory with the young boys Jack Kneedler and a friend. Kneedler & Sons was the contractor for the 1910 Kaw City School.

-MARCH-10-1913.-
RETURNING TRIP FROM
TIA JUANA-OLD MEXICO TO KAW, OKLA.

Graham Family Trip (1913)

The Graham family posed for photographs after driving to Yellowstone Park, WY, then down the coast of California into Mexico. They took tents to sleep in because there were no motels. They had to back their cars up the hills. Otherwise, the angle of their gas tanks wouldn't allow gas to get to the engines. They tied logs to the backs of the cars when they drove down steep hills to keep from going too fast. Family members included Car 1: Augusta, William, John and Martha. Car 2: Olive, O.B., George, and his wife. Car 3: Fulton, Ethel, Kerney and Vernel.

79

Eva Diamond (Circa 1910s)
Telephone operator Eva Diamond sits at the switchboard in Kaw City, ready to transfer incoming and outgoing phone calls.

Photo courtesy of John Krebs

Kaw City High School Orchestra (1912)
Kaw City Teachers and the High School Orchestra students. Back row (R-L): Tommy Smith and Bill Krebs *(other names unknown)*.

Smith's Dry Goods Store (Circa 1910)

Owner T.E. Smith stands in front of his Dry Goods Store. This was an early day department store selling a wide variety of household items and clothing.

Photo courtesy of Tom Trueblood

Kaw City Motor Company (Circa 1916)

The Kaw City Motor Company sold Lincoln, Ford and Fordson vehicles which included automobiles, trucks, farm machinery and tractors. The white frame building next door was the Lyle Hiner Furniture Store. It later became the White Front Filling Station and Garage, named because it was painted white.

Photo courtesy of Lillian Brill

U.S. Army Recruits (1917)
These young men posed for a photograph after enlisting in the U.S. Army during WWI. (L-R): John Elwell, Harry Kneedler, Guy Claybaugh, Harley Taylor, Clarence Kneedler, Mack Pellman, Nate Stevens and Frank Herbert.

Photo courtesy of Imogene Levitt

World War I Soldiers on Leave (1918)
Back (L-R): Guy Claybaugh and Clarence Kneedler. Front (L-R): Shorty
Noblet and Harry Kneedler.

Gus Joseph's Store (1920)
(L-R): Charlie Carriger, Billy Jones (Emma Monroe's father), Harry Grantham, Mr. Storns (sharpening the knife), Gus Joseph (owner) and Manser "Curly" Hughes (meat cutter).

Frank Hutchison's Kaw City Newspaper (1913)

The Kaw City News was owned by Frank Hutchison. An Eagle Drug Store Calendar on the wall is turned to January 1913. Standing is Jessie Rowell Rine. Seated (L-R): Lorne Scott, Unknown and Bill Krebs.

Photo courtesy of Maggie Lyon

Kaw City Baseball
This group of young men were members of the first baseball team in Kaw City.

Photo courtesy of Clyde Barker

Little Boys and Their Toys (Circa 1915)
Children enjoyed playing imaginary games outdoors. John Hoefer, Jr. *(left)* and Clyde Barker *(right)* even dressed up in costume.

Photo courtesy of Ollie Payne

Main Street Parade (Circa 1917)
People were lined up on the street to watch a parade of cars drive by. Some of the automobiles were decorated with streamers.

O.F. Schroke Store (1918)

The long, narrow store owned by O.F. Schroke sold mostly groceries. Behind the left counter, the front man is Unknown. Jack Kneedler is behind him. Mrs. Schroke is holding her daughter, Ruth in front of the left counter. Mr. Schroke is at the very back of the right counters. Bertha Randoll is the front woman behind the right counter.

Hutchison Pig Farm (1916)
Frank Hutchison and farm hands show off some of Frank's prize pigs.

Home of I.M. "Ike" and Laura Clubb (1918)
Ike Clubb stands in front of his house on Main Street.

Photo courtesy of Earl Malherbe

Frank Malherbe and Henry Laurent (Circa 1920s)

Photo courtesy of Mrs. J.E. Neill

J.E. Neill Hardware Store (1923)
Employee Lyle Mitchell *(left)* and owner of the hardware and appliance store, J. E. Neill *(right)*.

Murphy Horseshoeing (1922)

The Murphy Horseshoing barn was located on Fifth Avenue in between Main and Oak Streets. Even though the automobile was readily available, many people still relied on horses for transportation. Indoor plumbing had also been invented, but judging from the outhouses in this picture, not everyone had toilets in their homes.

Photo courtesy of Jack Kneedler

Main Street (1922)

East side of Main Street taken by Wichita, Kansas photographer J.D. Turley. Businesses from left to right: O.F. Schroke Grocery and Dry Goods Store, Unknown, Henry Diamond's Harness Shop and Electric Shoe Shop, Cafe, Barber Shop, Kaw City Bakery, Unknown and Woodman Hall. Woodman Hall was rolled on logs, moved from Longwood, OK to Kaw City. It was one of the first buildings in the town.

Photo courtesy of Jack Kneedler

F. B. Hutchison Groceries and Kaw Theater (1922)
Hutchison's Grocery Store was on Main Street. Next door, the Kaw Theatre was the second indoor theater to be built in the city. "The Town That Forgot God" was the current featured film.

Widney Children (1922)
Kenneth Widney, dressed in his Boy Scouts of America uniform, stands with sister Lois. Their father, J.T.B. Widney owned the Widney Drug Store.

Street Scene (1922)

Buildings beginning at top left: Santa Fe Hotel, The Midland Supply Company, Kaw Drug Company, Joe Liebenheim Exclusive Men's Store, Unknown, Preston's Variety Store, Hamburger Restaurant (*sign says "2 Good Places To Eat, Here and Home*), Drug Store and Popular Cafe (*one year after gas explosion*).

Photo courtesy of the Belmard Family

Pool Hall (1920)

The Pool Hall was often a gathering place for young men. Prohibition prevented the legal sale of alcohol, but tobacco was readily available. The handwritten sign hanging above the pool table says, "If you can't pay don't play!"

Charles Curtis on the Campaign Trail (1928)
Charles Curtis with his cousin Belle Auld at a campaign rally in Kaw City shortly becore he was elected
Vice President of the United States in November of 1928.

Photo courtesy of Glen Conklin

Ellen Irene Hayner Diamond (Circa 1920)
Ellen was married to Henry Diamond, owner of the Harness
Shop, one of the first businesses in Kaw City.

Main Street (Early 1920s)

Kaw City's streets were filled with automobiles in the early 1920s, but a close look shows some people still used horse-drawn wagons. First National Bank in Kaw City has a painted sign on their building *(left)*, boasting capital funds of $25,000.

Cramen Branch (Circa 1920s)
Cramen Branch played guard for a Kaw City basketball team sponsored by the American Legion.

The Old and the New (Circa 1920s)

Dr. Irvin stands beside his new car while his wife sits in their old buggy hitched to Pate the horse. Son Leon "Doodle Doc" sits behind the wheel of the car.

Photo courtesy of Jack Kneedler

Moose Lodge Carnival Promotion (1920)
A local band stops at the intersection of Fifth Avenue and Main Street to play music and advertise the upcoming Moose Lodge Carnival. On the left *(west)* side of Main Street is the F.H. Voils Meat Market.

Photo courtesy of Ollie Payne

Neill Hardware Delivery Truck (1922)
J.E. Neill sold Winchesters in his hardware store on Main Street.

Kaw City Motor Company (Circa 1920s)

Fords and luxury Lincoln automobiles were sold at the Kaw City Motor Company. Standing in front are some of the salesmen and mechanics.

Inside the Kaw City Motor Company (Circa 1920s)
Mechanics at work in the Kaw City Motor Company garage.

Growth on Main Street Continues (1922)

Soon after the Conklin Opera House was built in 1904, the north side was added onto. T.E. Smith's store on the lower level carried Nelly Don dresses, Brown shoes, bulk fabric and sewing supplies. Apartments were on the second floor. South of the Opera House, Neill Hardware was built. The first level was the store and the Neill family lived above it. On the corner, supplies have been delivered for the construction of I.M. Clubb's building which would house multiple businesses and offices.

Kaw City Sand Company Truck (1922)

The Kaw City Sand Company delivered washed river sand. Phone numbers were only three digits in the early days. All you had to do was call the operator and ask for "1-7-4" to reach the Sand Company.

Oil Derrick (Circa 1920s)

Drilling for oil was hard work but there was a lot of oil to be discovered in the land north and east of Kaw City beyond the Arkansas River. This picture shows Jack Kneedler's oil derrick and power station, busy with workers.

Feagins Drug Store (1922)

Ed Lewis built the first drugstore when Kaw City was established. In the early 1920s, the name was changed to Feagins Drug Store when Mr. and Mrs. Feagin *(right)* bought it.

Kaw City Boy's Basketball Team (1922)
(L-R): Joe Baum, Loyd Null, Percy Smith, Mill Emrick, Gerald Hickman, Forrest Overman and Carl Duval. Coach's name Unknown.

Interior of I.M. "Ike" and Laura Clubb's Home (Early 1920s)
Laura Clubb's vast art collection of master paintings was displayed on the walls of her Kaw City home until she ran out of wall space. The paintings were moved to the Clubb Hotel where people came from around the world to see them.

Laura Clubb (Early 1920s)

Art collector Laura Clubb in her Kaw City home prior to the paintings relocation in the Clubb Hotel. Three decades later, most of her collection was donated to the Philbrook Art Museum in Tulsa, OK.

Kaw City's Municipal Electric Light & Power Plant (1921)
Kaw City's fire truck is parked outside of the Fire Station which was a part of the Power Plant. The city alarm, used for fires, floods, tornadoes, etc. was located there also.

Nichols Garage (Circa 1925)
Owned by the Nichols family, this shop repaired everything from cars to furniture.

Photo courtesy of Lillian Brill

Kaw City School (1922)

Kaw City's School was enlarged in 1922 to accommodate a growing number of students. The large building on the right included an auditorium, stage, dressing rooms, study hall and library. Attached on the left side was a building that housed the office and High School classes.

Kaw City Main Street (1922)
The First National Bank is featured in the center of this picture on the corner. Two doors down from it is Kaw City's first Post Office.

Kaw Natatorium
The swimming pool and skating rink at Kaw Natatorium were owned by "Happy" Howard.

Burtscher's Produce House
Owner Otto Burtscher *(left)* stands in front of his Produce House. Jack Kneedler is next to him.

Booster Parade (1922)
The Kaw City Boosters traveled through the streets of surrounding towns honking and advertising Kaw City as a great community to live in.

W.T. Conklin Grocery Store (1925)

Mrs. Mary Ellen Diamond Conklin operated the family grocery store with the help of her two youngest sons, Glen *(left)* and Hugo *(right)*. The calendar on the wall is dated July 1925.

Brush Building (Circa 1920s)

The Brush Building, located on Fifth Avenue, provided gasoline and auto services. The car on the left is a 1928 Model A. The car on the right is a 1925 Model T.

Kaw City Motor Company Outdoor Showroom (1922)
The Kaw City Motor Company owned by Coleman Peters parked its automobile inventory across the street from their business. The two children in front of the fourth car from the right are Mary Elizabeth and her brother Ikie Lynn Clubb.

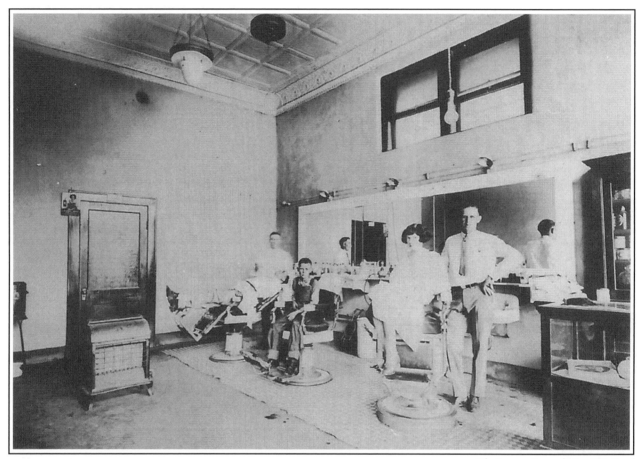

Tom Ford Barber Shop (1924)

In 1924, Tom Ford's Barber Shop was on Fifth Avenue across the street from Kaw City's second Post Office. He later moved the shop to Main Street between Fifth and Sixth Avenue facing east. Mr. Ford is on the right with his wife Judy in the chair. One of their three sons is in the middle chair.

Thompson-Parker Lumber Company (1922)

Kaw City was a booming small town. One sign of growth was multiple lumber yards like Thompson-Parker Lumber Company providing wood and building supplies. It was located in the northeastern quadrant of Kaw City.

Photo courtesy of Carolyn Godberson

Wolfe Brothers Store (1913)

Many of the businesses along Main Street were narrow and deep. The Wolfe Brothers Store operated by Lonnie and Charlie Wolfe sold groceries and dry goods.

Photo courtesy of Jack Kneedler

American Lumber Company (1922)
The American Lumber Company was located in northeast Kaw City near its competitor, Thompson-Parker Lumber Company.

Hotel Kaw (1922)
The Hotel Kaw faced north on the east side of Fifth Avenue.

The Home Furniture Company (1922)

Irene and Lyle Hiner stand in front of their furniture store with daughter Harriet and 3-year-old son Harold. Kaw City Plumbing was next door, run by Mr. Emerick.

Storefronts (1922)

The Grantham & Ramsey Store was on the corner of Main Street and Fifth Avenue next door to F.B. Hutchison Groceries. Businesses and residences are visible in the background. This bird's eye view was probably captured from the top of the bank building across the street.

Photo courtesy of Lorene Gingerich

Jesse Willis Drug Store (Circa 1926)
(L to R): Muriel Fronkier, Temple McQuirk, Bernice Ledeker and druggist John Strickland.

Photo courtesy of Ed Lewis

South Bridge Rescue Efforts (1923)

Kaw City men did everything they could to save the south bridge during the flood of 1923. They tried to remove the driftwood that kept building up, but the bridge finally gave way to the high waters. Both the south and north bridges were lost in the flood. Only the north bridge was rebuilt. Ferries and a swinging walk bridge were used during the rebuilding of the north bridge way.

Photo courtesy of Louise Burgert

Flood on Main Street (1923)
A view of the Main Street flooding. The water was waist-high on grown men.

Flood on Main Street (1923)
A view of the flood waters on Main Street looking northeast.

Flood on Main Street (1923)
As the flood waters receded, some of the gentlemen enjoyed swimming in the streets.

Kaw City Flood (1923)
Another view of flooded Main Street buildings. O.B. Graham's Mechanic Shop is the building on the right.

Photo courtesy of Jack Kneedler

Kaw City Flood (1923)
Partially submerged cars were stranded along Fifth Avenue. This view is looking east.

Flood Damage (1923)

The flood temporarily halted trains from coming into Kaw City when it washed the railroad out east of town on June 11, 1923. This photo was taken looking east from the C.F. Kneedler farm house.

Buildings Decimated in the Flood (1923)
The American Lumber Company on the northeast side of Kaw City was heavily damaged along with all the buildings surrounding it.

Standing on the Foot Bridge (1923)

A swinging foot bridge was constructed when the bridge crossing the Arkansas River north of Kaw City was washed out. This bridge, personal canoes and a ferry were the only ways people could cross to the other side of the river to get to their homes, farms, schools and Washunga. One of the old bridge "bents" is visible just beyond the foot bridge.

Photo courtesy of Jack Kneedler

Foot Bridge (1923)
This is the view from the Kaw City side of the swinging foot bridge looking north towards Washunga.

Waiting For the Ferry (1923)
After the north bridge washed out, the ferry stayed busy, carrying wagons, automobiles and people from one side of the Arkansas River to the other. These people are waiting for their turn to cross.

Ferry Boat Ride (1923)
The ferry was tethered to a line that crossed from one side of the Arkansas River to the other.

Ferry Across Arkansas River (1923)
Wooden docks were built so the ferry could load and off-load people and vehicles. This picture gives you an idea how many wagons and cars could fit onto the ferry at one time. They probably had numerous traffic jams!

Photo courtesy of Pete and Ramona Auld

Washunga Station (Early 1920s)

The Washunga Gas Station was north of the Arkansas River on the road from Kaw City leading into Washunga. It was owned and operated by James and Belle Pappan Auld *(left)*. Pictured with them is Silas Conn *(right)*.

Photo courtesy of R.W. Cline

Trip to Colorado (1927)
A group of Kaw Citians went on a road trip to Pikes Peak, Colorado. Pictured in the middle seat are Lavern and Dora Cline. Mrs. Cline is holding 22-month-old son Robert.

Kaw City Girl's Basketball Team (1924)
Front (L-R): Teacher Vivian Montgomery, Velda Rundle, Amy Riddle and Unknown. Middle (L-R): Kathryn Black, Edith Montgomery, Ramona Rutherford and Violet Grantham. Back (L-R): Della Mae, Minnie Riddle, Lillian Myers and Ellen Conklin.

Photo courtesy of R.W. Cline

Out For a Ride (Circa 1920s)

Women were rarely seen without dresses except when they dressed for trips in the automobile. Shown above are Lavern Cline and wife, Dora Ellen Cline, Flora Cline and husband, Bill Cline.

Photo courtesy of Jack Kneedler

Kaw City Residences (1922)
This is a rooftop view of the houses on the block east of Main Street between Fifth and Sixth Avenues.

Photo courtesy of Glen Conklin

Construction Crew (1923)
This group of men were the workers who built the Clubb Hotel.

Photo courtesy of Leon Irvin

Clubb Hotel and Bank Under Construction (1923)
Workmen took a break from building the hotel to pose for a picture. Materials were purchased from Thompson-Parker Lumber Company, a local Kaw City business. The building was so soundly constructed that 50 years later when it was to be demolished, dynamite blasts broke little more than its picture windows and front glassed entry.

Clubb Hotel and Bank (1924)

The multi-level building on Main Street housing the Clubb Hotel was built by Ike Clubb in 1924. It included three stories plus a large mezzanine floor. One fourth of the lower level on the corner was occupied by the National Bank of Kaw City.

Photo courtesy of Glen Conklin

Clubb Hotel Lobby (1924)

The lovely Clubb Hotel lobby was a comfortable place to sit and relax. An elevator, located to the right of the stairs, made getting up to the upper floors convenient for guests.

Clubb Hotel Dining Room (1924)
The Clubb Hotel offered fine dining seven days a week for many years. It served both hotel patrons and walk-in guests.

National Bank of Kaw City (Circa 1925)

The interior of the National Bank of Kaw City, located in the lower northeast quadrant of the Clubb Hotel, matched the decor of the hotel's Lobby and Dining Room. Bank officers Hugo Milde and C. L. Shidler are seated in the front cubicle.

Photo courtesy of Jack Kneedler

Harness Shop (1922)

The Harness and Electric Shoe Shop on Main Street was owned and operated by Henry Diamond. Next door to it was a cafe, a barber shop and the Kaw City Bakery.

Photo courtesy of Page Manley

Kaw City Senior Class Picture (1928)
Back (L-R): Paul Carringer, Mearl Fronkier, Leslie Brown, Nolan Shupe, Ernest Riddle, John Bowman and John Grantham. Middle (L-R): Beverly Simpson, Clarence Blair, Sara Smith, Jesse Jones, Catherine Kelso, Boyd Fesler and Geraldine Shidler. Front (L-R): Rowena Smith, Frances Sine, Pearl Ivy, Mr. and Mrs. Manley, Marie Brown and Lois Widney.

Horse-Drawn Wagon (Circa 1920s)

This wagon is typical of the wagons and horses that carried oil field supplies and equipment from Kaw City to the Burbank Oil Fields. The horses are wearing fly nets that helped keep the flies away.

Jim Barker Store (1928)
Jim Barker stands next to his son in their store. He sold shoes, hats, mens and women's clothing and dry goods.

Conklin Brothers (1925)

W.T. Conklin and two of his brothers Min and Mose, pose for a family photograph. Mustaches, vests, pocket watches, high collars and Derby hats were the style of the period.

Eagle Garage (1929)

The Eagle Garage was on Main Street across from the city park. Standing in front are Jesse Hoisington and owner L.E. Cook.

Julie Pappan (Circa 1920s)
Julie Gonvil Pappan and granddaughter Isabelle "Belle" Pappan. Julie was Vice President Charles Curtis' Grandmother. Charles Curtis spent a great deal of time with her in Washunga as a child.

Photo courtesy of Mary Ellen Conklin

Kaw Citians Attend Inauguration (1929)

The train travelers pictured above are part of a large group of people invited to attend the Hoover and Curtis inauguration in 1929. (R-L): Unknown, Unknown, Mr. Littlewalker and Son, Unknown, Unknown, Mrs. Littlewalker, Belle Auld *(Charles Curtis' cousin)*, Pawnee Bill, Unknown, Ike Clubb and Hugo Milde.

Charity "Chattie" Alice Tipton and Augusta Clubb (Early 1920s)
Augusta Graham Clubb *(right)* had a millinery shop in Kaw City in the early 1920s and made beautiful hats of all sizes and shapes.

The Baughman Lumber Company

Mr. Kellam and his son-in-law, John Jarmolowitz stand in front of their business. They repaired and sold Norge Rollator Refrigerators, tools and radios.

J.E. Neill Hardware Store (Circa 1920s)

Bill Ballaugh is on the left and owner J.E. Neill is on the right in Neill's hardware store. As evidenced in the photograph, they sold a little of everything.

Fifth & 6th Grade Class Picture (1934)

Back (L-R): Junior Ashton, Jack Robinson, Cashish Tull, Delbert Slack and Junior Reed. 4th Row (L-R): Frankie Smith, Eugene Moreland, Lona Jennings, Audrey Tharp, Esther Robinson, Jacqueline Walton, Jetina Stevenson, Ruth Carr, Betty Williams, Lillie Morgan and Teacher Miss Hosford. 3rd Row (L-R): Ethel Taylor, Edna Bartles, June Foust, Imogene McClintock, Glenda Bowman, Mary Hart, Juanita Rafferty, Margie Manning, Nona Peters, Barbara Lukins. 2nd Row (L-R): Owen Carr, Jack Hodges, Homer Breece, Paul Roberts, Ikie Lynn Clubb, Robert Johnson, Charles King, Freddie Wall, Kenton Kurtz, Donald Hutchinson and Glenn Rogers. Front (L-R): Margaret Collins, Martha Willis, Louis Houser, Elmo Rogers, Orvalee Hoisington, Bessie Taylor, Margaret Ingraham, Mable Calkins, and Martha Wilson.

Telephone Switchboard (Circa 1930s)
Operator Mary Jo Roberts sits at the telephone switchboard ready to answer and connect callers. The telephone office was located on the second floor of the National Bank of Kaw City.

Alice Summers, Ike Clubb and Silas Conn (Circa 1930s)
Alice Summers and Silas Conn stand at the side of Ike Clubb sitting in his famous elk chair in front of the Clubb Hotel. Blind Silas spent hours every day sitting in a shaded area on Main Street. People often stopped to talk to him. Even though he was blind, he claimed to know who they were by the sound of their walk.

Clubb Hotel Lobby (1938)

Some of Laura Clubb's art collection is visible in the lobby and hallway leading to the dining room along with Ike Clubb's collection of longhorn, moose and deer heads. Furniture from the Clubb Hotel can be viewed in the Kaw City Museum.

Redhawk Football Team (1936)
Back (L-R): Roger Conn, Wilbur Hubler, Harold Randall, Dick Gilby, Harold Yager and Coach Bob White. Middle (L-R): Jack Cross, Carl Rafferty, Dean Manning, Bill Yeoman and Francis Hodges. Front (L-R): Elroy Boxley, Earl Boxley, Steve Cross and Eugene Parker.

Photo courtesy of L.M. Cline

Robert W. "Bob" Cline (1934)
9-year-old Cowboy Bob riding his Shetland Pony.

W.O. Whitlock (Circa 1930s)

Mr. Whitlock stands beside his parked hearse in front of his Kaw City home. He owned Whitlock and Sons Furniture Store and operated a funeral home in the back of the building.

Rundle Grocery Store (1926-1935)

Jess Rundle is pictured in his grocery store located at Fifth Avenue and Main Street in the old bank building. Part of the ceiling *(left back)* has ripped and is held up with tape. A few years later, Rundle relocated to a different location on Main Street.

Photo courtesy of Jack Kneedler

Gem Theater (Circa 1930s)
The Gem Theater was the first indoor movie theater in Kaw City. Standing in front are owners C.F. Kneedler Sr. and C.F. Kneedler Jr.

Photo courtesy of Emma Randol

Dean Randol, Chief of Police (Early 1930s)

Kaw City Grade School and High School (1938)
Built in 1910, the classrooms in this large two-story building accommodated first through eighth grade Kaw City students.

Kaw City High School Band (1942)
Row 4 (L-R) Helen Reynolds, Billy Rogers, Unknown, John Guy Widney, Bobby Branch, Castner Scott, Robert Johnson, Donley Ford, Billy Lyons and Joe Bob Ingraham. Row 3 (L-R): Annette Conklin Cline Pittman, Donald Cline, Robert Cline, Melba June Howard, Orvalee Hoisington, Martha Ann Walcott, Charlene Parker, Leona Springer Scott and Helen Miller. Row 2 (L-R): O.W. Wilton, Patsy Whitlock, Mary Ellen Cross, Thomasine Smith, Louis Reynolds, Lewis Branch, Leonard Hart, Roy Dean Schmitt or Paul Fanske. Row 1 (L-R): Charlene Gay, Mary Belle Auld, Harry Joe Gaston, Ileen Wilson, Darlene McClintock, Joan Bryson and Donna Jo Parker.

Photo courtesy of Maggie Lyon

Mr. and Mrs. Price Benton (Circa 1940s)

Photo courtesy of Jack Kneedler

I.M. Clubb Building (Circa 1924-1930)

The I.M. Clubb building on the corner was built in 1922. A Meat Market and Gus Joseph's General Merchandise Store were in the front half of the ground floor. This later became the Whitlock and Sons Furniture Store. The newspaper office faced the side street. Offices were on the second floor including the telephone office for awhile. At different times, the Independent Order of Odd Fellows and Masons met in this building.

Senior Class Play (1942)
(R-L): Orvalee Hoisington, Leonard Springer, Robert Johnson, Fern Dick, Bessie Dilworth, Tommy Holmes, Fred Wall, Mabel Calkins, Charles Pittman and Betty Rooks.

Flood on Main Street (1945)

Two more big floods hit Kaw City after the Flood of 1923. One in the fall of 1943, and then one in the spring of 1945. This picture shows Willis Grocery and Market filled with flood waters from the Arkansas River.

Kaw City Flood (1943)
Flooded houses and businesses on the west side of the park.

Photo courtesy of Orvalee Hoisington

Kaw City Flood (1945)
Flooding on Fifth Avenue and beyond. The Kaw Poultry House, just west of Main Street was completely flooded.

Rundle Grocery Store (1940)
Jess Rundle is pictured on the right in his new grocery story which was in the middle of the block on the west side of Main Street.

Photo courtesy of Lillian Brill

First Methodist Church (1942)

First Methodist Church completed this building in 1925. Their parsonage was the white frame house located next door.

Photo courtesy of Glen Conklin

Free Barbecue (1942)
The Conklin Elevator furnished Purina-fed pigs for a city-wide barbecue. Cars were parked solid for blocks around as people took full advantage of a free meal!

Photo courtesy of Mrs. J.E. Neill

Johnny Guy Widney (1943)
Johnny Guy Widney took flying lessons in Ponca City, then enlisted in the US Air Force on October 26, 1943. Less than one year later, the plane he was flying exploded and he was killed.

Photo courtesy of G.G. Conklin

Philbook Dinner Honoring Laura Clubb (1947)

The Philbrook Museum in Tulsa, Oklahoma held a dinner honoring Laura Clubb for her donation of a world-famous art collection to the museum. Beginning at front left: Mary Ellen Clubb, Glenda Sue Conklin Noval Thomas, Philbrook Curator's Wife, Ikie Lynn Clubb, Lodema Rutherford, Philbrook Board Member, Laura Clubb, Mr. A.J. Hurt (Procurement Officer for Philbrook Museum), Madelyn Clubb Conklin, Valentine Rutherford Dimmit, Eloise Dimmit, Mary Ellen Diamond Conklin, Museum Curator, Annette Conklin Cline Pittman, Glen Conklin and Mrs. A.J. Hurt.

Photo courtesy of R.W. Cline

The Last Train Stop (1971)

Kaw City schools released students so they could turn out to watch the last train stop in Kaw City before that section of the line was closed down in preparation for the Kaw Dam construction. However, heavy rains in Oklahoma flooded other tracks and the only way for the train to bypass the flooding was to be re-routed through Kaw City. Unexpectedly, people were awakened in the middle of the night to hear that old familiar sound of their train rumbling by one more time.

KAW CITY DEPOT TO BE MOVED

The last days of old Kaw City are fast coming to an end. The Kaw Dam Project has forced the relocation of the town to a site two miles west of its present location. Plans are now under way to move the old Santa Fe Railroad station to a spot near the Municipal building in the new town. The Atchison, Topeka, and Santa Fe Railway Company has officially donated the depot "to be utilized as a museum for historical documents and exhibits of the early pioneering days of the community."

The station was begun late in 1902 as the Eastern Oklahoma Railway Company was in the process of building a railroad line from Newkirk to Pauls Valley, and was completed in February, 1903. At the time it was built, it was the finest station on the new line, having a platform on the south, or passenger side, of 270 feet and on the north side of about 90 feet, giving ample accomodations for the extensive freight business which was expected.

During the early life of the railroad, thousands of bushels of corn and other farm products were moved to the market place, and hundreds of carloads of Texas cattle were moved into the bountiful grazing lands of the Osage for fattening prior to moving them on to market. It was a rich agricultural area and the gateway to the Kaw and Osage reservations. In later years, the railroad moved oil field equipment into the area as the fabulous Burbank Oil field came into being.

The railroad and the people of Kaw worked together for the common good and the area prospered for many years. No one could anticipate the tragedy which was to befall the town in the form of the raging waters of the Arkansas river during the spring of 1923. The flood inundated much of the town and destroyed both the north and south bridges, which were vital arteries for trade. In order to continue to supply the needs of the growing areas "across the river" the railroad found it necessary to establish new supply points beyond the Arkansas, bypassing the once proud and flourishing commuity of Kaw. It is ironic that these same waters, backed up by the Kaw Dam, now under construction, will again cover the town of Kaw.

The Santa Fe Depot, which served as such a vital part of the early community, will be the only surviving business building of the old town.

Funds to move and restore the old depot will be derived entirely from donations of those interested in preserving the heritage of the early days in the "Ox Bow Bend." Donations of time, labor, and materials will also be needed as the move gets under way this coming month. Anyone desiring to share in the project may send donations to Kaw City in care of the museum fund. Those in the Ponca City area desiring more information on the project may call 762-3046.

Photo courtesy of R.W. Cline

Fund-Raising Letter (1971)
Letter sent by Bob Cline to raise money for moving and preserving the Kaw City Depot.

Deeding the Depot to the Kaw City Museum (1971)

The Kaw City Museum Association was organized by some of the town's citizens to help preserve the history of old Kaw City. Mayor Fred Munson was assigned to acquire the depot building from the railroad company so it could be moved to the new townsite and become a musuem. Mayor Munson *(above)* gratefully accepted the deed to the depot from a railroad representative on the condition that after the depot was moved, the land would be cleared and left in good condition. The Kaw City Museum Association was more than happy to comply. The combination safe behind Munson is on exhibit at the Kaw City Museum.

First Christian Church (1971)
The First Christian Church on Main Street. The steeple above the entry has been removed.

Rundle's Grocery Store (1971)
Jess Rundle stands at the counter in his grocery store, one of the few businesses still open in Kaw City in 1971.

Photo courtesy of Corps of Engineers

Jailhouse (1972)

In the early days, a jailhouse was called a calaboose, taken from the Spanish word calabozo which means "dungeon". Kaw City's calaboose consisted of little more than two individual cells, not the most desirable of accommodations.

Photo courtesy of R.W. Cline

Methodist Church Ruins (1972)
This photo was taken of the Methodist Church during its demolition by the Corps of Engineers.

Moving the Depot (1972)

A parade on May 13, 1972 celebrated Kaw City's final day in its original location. The depot and its outhouse were supposed to be the last two floats in the parade, but the depot was too tall to drive under power lines by the city park. It would have to be moved at a later date. In the meantime, Uncle Sam was on hand to direct traffic.

Outhouse Parade Float (1972)
The depot's outhouse with children on the roof and inside was the last float of the final day parade.

Photo courtesy of R.W. Cline

Kaw City Museum (1978)

The Depot was successfully moved to the town's new location and re-purposed as the Kaw City Museum. In the beginning, only two rooms were open to the public. The freight room was unfinished and used for storage. The outhouse was also cleaned up and repainted, but never again used for a relief station.

New Kaw City (1973)

This aerial view of the new Kaw City was taken by the Corps of Engineers. The new water tower can be seen in the distance, as well as buildings and residences that either moved from the old town or were newly built.

Photo courtesy of R.W. Cline

Kaw City Museum (1980)

Layer upon layer of paint had to be scraped off the old depot before the exterior of the building could be painted. The tedious project took time, but the end result was a beautiful red building trimmed in white. Bricks from the old platform were used to create a new front porch, supported by a retaining wall made from old railroad ties.

Kenneth and Brunella Brill (Early 1990s)

Kenneth Brill was reared and schooled in old Kaw City but spent much of his career in Denver, Colorado where he retired. Though he was gone from Kaw City for many years, he never forgot where he came from. He continued to take part in Kaw City reunions and when the museum needed to expand, he was the first to donate to its building fund. His continued participation and donation of major financial support enabled the Kaw City Museum to build a new addition, The Kenneth W. Brill Building, which was dedicated on May 28, 1995.

Kaw City Museum (2017)

Kaw City Museum is the only surviving commercial building from the original Kaw City townsite. In 1979 it was added to Oklahoma's National Register of Historical Places and the National Register of Historic Places. The museum is open for visitors on the weekends during summer months and hosts an annual reunion every Memorial Weekend. Historical records, objects, photographs, clothing, furniture and artifacts donated by the men and women who grew up in Kaw City rival the exhibits of any museum in the region. Operating on donations and run by volunteers, Kaw City Museum continues to fulfill its vision of preserving the history of a town that was washed away but will never be forgotten.

If you would like to receive updates about Kaw City Museum go to kawcitymuseum.com and subscribe.

Index

Alice Summers, Ike Clubb and Silas Conn (Circa 1930s) --- 173
American Lumber Company (1922) --- 131
Armstrong Restaurant and Rock Island Machine Shop (1912) --- 76
Bandstand (Circa 1911) --- 62
Bank of Commerce (Early 1900s) --- 43
Barnum Family (Circa 1900) --- 44
Bert Fleharty (1902) --- 21
B.F. "Bill" Smith Hardware Store (Circa 1905) --- 53
Blacksmith DeBolt (Circa 1906) --- 33
Booster Parade (1922) --- 124
Brush Building (Circa 1920s) --- 126
Buildings Decimated in the Flood (1923) --- 143
Building the Bridge (1903) --- 24
Burtscher's Produce House --- 123
Cattle Drive (Circa 1870s) --- 9
Cement Block Factory (1911) --- 78
Charles Curtis on the Campaign Trail (1928) --- 102
Cherokee Strip Land Run (1893) --- 13
Clubb Hotel and Bank (1924) --- 156
Clubb Hotel and Bank Under Construction (1923) --- 155
Clubb Hotel Dining Room (1924) --- 158
Clubb Hotel Lobby (1924) --- 157
Clubb Hotel Lobby (1938) --- 174
Clubb Ranch (Early 1910s) --- 60
Clyde Sharp (Circa 1903) --- 19
Clyde Sharp Livery --- 40
Conklin Brothers (1925) --- 164
Conklin Opera House (1904) --- 56
Construction Crew (1923) --- 154
Cox Wedding (1903) --- 28
Cramen Branch (Circa 1920s) --- 105
Crossing the Arkansas River (1895) --- 17
Dean Randol, Chief of Police (Early 1930s) --- 180
Deeding the Depot to the Kaw City Museum (1971) --- 196
Eagle Garage (1929) --- 165
Early Day Home (Early 1900s) --- 61
Early Day Hunter (Late 1800s) --- 14
Early Days on Main Street (Early 1900s) --- 39
Early Day Transportation (Circa 1903) --- 55
Early Settler Dugout (1894) --- 16
Edwards Tailor and Cleaning Shop (Circa 1910s) --- 64

Index

Edwards Tailor and Cleaning Shop (Circa 1910s) --------------- 65
Eighth Grade Student Class Picture (1908) ------------------- 54
Ellen Irene Hayner Diamond (Circa 1920) --------------------- 103
Eva Diamond (Circa 1910s) ---------------------------------- 80
Farmers (1872) -- 10
Farmers National Bank of Kaw City (1911) ------------------- 70
Farmers National Bank of Kaw City (1911) ------------------- 71
Farm Machinery (Early 1900s) ------------------------------- 30
F. B. Hutchison Groceries and Kaw Theater (1922) ----------- 98
Feagins Drug Store (1922) ---------------------------------- 114
Feagin's Drugstore (Circa 1915) ---------------------------- 74
Ferguson Family (Late 1800s) ------------------------------- 15
Ferry Across Arkansas River (1923) ------------------------- 148
Ferry Boat Ride (1923) ------------------------------------- 147
Fifth & 6th Grade Class Picture (1934) --------------------- 171
First Christian Church (1971) ------------------------------ 197
First Christian Church (Early 1900s) ----------------------- 57
First Methodist Church (1904-1912) ------------------------- 41
First Methodist Church (1912-1925) ------------------------- 72
First Methodist Church (1942) ------------------------------ 190
First State Bank of Kaw City (1909) ------------------------ 59
Flood Damage (1923) -- 142
Flood on Main Street (1923) -------------------------------- 137
Flood on Main Street (1923) -------------------------------- 138
Flood on Main Street (1923) -------------------------------- 139
Flood on Main Street (1945) -------------------------------- 186
Foot Bridge (1923) --- 145
Frank Hutchison's Kaw City Newspaper (1913) ---------------- 87
Frank Malherbe and Henry Laurent (Circa 1920s) ------------- 94
Free Barbecue (1942) --------------------------------------- 191
Fund-Raising Letter (1971) --------------------------------- 195
Gem Theater (Circa 1930s) ---------------------------------- 179
Graham Family Trip (1913) ---------------------------------- 79
Growth on Main Street Continues (1922) --------------------- 111
Gus Joseph's Store (1920) ---------------------------------- 86
Guy Family Picture (1868) ---------------------------------- 8
Harness Shop (1922) -- 160
Headed to Town (Early 1900s) ------------------------------- 29
H.E. Guy Home (1910) --------------------------------------- 58
Home of I.M. "Ike" and Laura Clubb (1918) ------------------ 93
Home of W.T. and Mary Ellen Conklin (Circa 1907) ----------- 49

Index

Horse-Drawn Wagon (Circa 1920s) ---- 162
Hotel Herman (1903) --34
Hotel Kaw (1922) -- 132
Hutchison Pig Farm (1916) --92
Ike Clubb and Friend (1883) --11
I.M. Clubb Building (Circa 1924-1930) -- 184
Inside the Kaw City Motor Company (Circa 1920s) -- 110
Interior of I.M. "Ike" and Laura Clubb's Home (Early 1920s) -- 116
Jailhouse (1972) -- 199
J.E. Neill Hardware Store (1923) --95
J.E. Neill Hardware Store (Circa 1920s) -- 170
Jesse Willis Drug Store (Circa 1926) -- 135
Jim Barker Store (1928) -- 163
Johnny Guy Widney (1943) -- 192
Julie Pappan (Circa 1920s) -- 166
Kaw Citians Attend Inauguration (1929) -- 167
Kaw City Baseball --88
Kaw City Boy's Basketball Team (1922) -- 115
Kaw City Depot (1917) --75
Kaw City Flood (1923) -- 140
Kaw City Flood (1923) -- 141
Kaw City Flood (1943) -- 187
Kaw City Flood (1945) -- 188
Kaw City Girl's Basketball Team (1924) -- 151
Kaw City Grade School and High School (1938) -- 181
Kaw City High School Band (1942) -- 182
Kaw City High School Orchestra (1912) --81
Kaw City Main Street (1922) -- 121
Kaw City Main Street (Circa 1904) --32
Kaw City Main Street (Circa 1908) --50
Kaw City Main Street (Circa 1910s) --67
Kaw City Military Band (1911) --73
Kaw City Motor Company (Circa 1916) --83
Kaw City Motor Company (Circa 1920s) -- 109
Kaw City Motor Company Outdoor Showroom (1922) -- 127
Kaw City Museum (1978) -- 203
Kaw City Museum (1980) -- 205
Kaw City Museum (2017) -- 207
Kaw City Post Office (Circa 1903) --52
Kaw City Residences (1922) -- 153
Kaw City Sand Company Truck (1922) -- 112

Index

Kaw City School (1922)-- 120
Kaw City Senior Class Picture (1928)-- 161
Kaw City's Municipal Electric Light & Power Plant (1921)------------------------- 118
Kaw City's Second School House (1904)--37
Kaw City Townsite Company (Early 1900s) --20
Kaw City Train Depot (Early 1900s) --35
Kaw Natatorium -- 122
Kenner Family (Circa 1910s)--69
Kenneth and Brunella Brill (Early 1990s)--- 206
Laura Clubb (Early 1920s) --- 117
Little Boys and Their Toys (Circa 1915) --89
Log Cabin in Cherokee Outlet (Circa 1890s) --12
Main Street (1922)---97
Main Street (Circa 1904)--26
Main Street (Early 1920s)--- 104
Main Street Garage (Circa 1910s) --68
Main Street Parade (Circa 1917) --90
Map of Kaw City (1910) --- 7
Methodist Church Ruins (1972) -- 200
Millinery Shop (Circa 1905)--51
Moose Lodge Carnival Promotion (1920)--- 107
Moving the Depot (1972) --- 201
Moving the Hay (Circa 1910s) --66
Mr. and Mrs. Price Benton (Circa 1940s) -- 183
Mrs. Dossett and Friends (Circa 1916) --77
Murphy Horseshoeing (1922) --96
National Bank of Kaw City (Circa 1925) --- 159
Neill Hardware Delivery Truck (1922) --- 108
New Kaw City (1973) -- 204
Nichols Garage (Circa 1925) --- 119
O.F. Schroke Store (1918) --91
Oil Derrick (Circa 1920s)--- 113
Ortho and Maxine Harvey (1915)--63
Out For a Ride (Circa 1920s) --- 152
Out For a Walk (1906) --47
Outhouse Parade Float (1972) -- 202
Pellman Chickens (Early 1900s)--25
Philbook Dinner Honoring Laura Clubb (1947)---------------------------------- 193
Pool Hall (1920)-- 101
Railroad Gang (1902) --22
Randoll Livery (1908) --45

Index

Redhawk Football Team (1936) --------- 175
Robert W. "Bob" Cline (1934) --------- 176
Ruby Irons (Early 1900s) --------- 38
Rundle Grocery Store (1926-1935) --------- 178
Rundle Grocery Store (1940) --------- 189
Rundle's Grocery Store (1971) --------- 198
Senior Class Play (1942) --------- 185
Smith's Dry Goods Store (Circa 1910) --------- 82
South Bridge Rescue Efforts (1923) --------- 136
Standing on the Foot Bridge (1923) --------- 144
Storefronts (1922) --------- 134
Street Scene (1922) --------- 100
Taylor Bar (Circa 1905) --------- 27
Telephone Switchboard (Circa 1930s) --------- 172
The Baughman Lumber Company --------- 169
The Home Furniture Company (1922) --------- 133
The Last Train Stop (1971) --------- 194
The Old and the New (Circa 1920s) --------- 106
The Wedding Gift (1909) --------- 48
Thompson-Parker Lumber Company (1922) --------- 129
Threshing Fields (Early 1900s) --------- 31
Tom Ford Barber Shop (1924) --------- 128
Trip to Colorado (1927) --------- 150
U.S. Army Recruits (1917) --------- 84
Waiting For the Ferry (1923) --------- 146
Waiting for the Ferry (Circa 1902) --------- 23
Washunga Station (Early 1920s) --------- 149
West Side School House (Circa 1900) --------- 18
Widney Children (1922) --------- 99
W.J. Krebs and Family (Circa 1902) --------- 36
W.J. Krebs Newsroom (Circa 1902) --------- 42
Wolfe Brothers Store (1913) --------- 130
World War I Soldiers on Leave (1918) --------- 85
W.O. Whitlock (Circa 1930s) --------- 177
W.T. Conklin Grain Company (1908) --------- 46
W.T. Conklin Grocery Store (1925) --------- 125

Made in the USA
Columbia, SC
20 July 2021